Judaism

Sue Penney

Heinemann Library
Chicago, Illinois

Designed by Ken Vail Graphic Design
Originated by Universal
Printed by Wing King Tong in Hong Kong.

05 04 03 02 01
10 9 8 7 6 5 4 3 2 1

Library of Congress Cataloging-in-Publication Data

Penney, Sue.
    Judaism / Sue Penney.
       p. cm. – (World beliefs and cultures)
    Includes bibliographical references and index.
    Summary: An overview of the beliefs and customs of Judaism, including an introduction to sacred texts, a history of the religion, important holidays, and worship practices around the world.
    ISBN 1-57572-358-1 (lib. bdg.)
    1. Judaism—Juvenile literature. [1. Judaism.] I. Title. II. Series.

BM573.P46 2000
296—dc21

                          00-023230

Acknowledgments
The Publishers would like to thank the following for permission to reproduce photographs:
AKG/Erich Lessing, p. 9; Ancient Art and Architecture, p. 24; Andes Press Agency/Carlos Reyes-Manzo, pp. 26a, 39, 42; Circa Photo Library, pp. 16, 28, Circa Photo Library/Barrie Searle, pp. 7, 12, 22, 37, Circa Photo Library/John Smith, p. 15, Circa Photo Library/Zbigniew Kosc, p. 41; Collections/ Mike Kipling, p. 10; Impact Photos/Robin Laurance, p. 23; Impact Photos/Rachel Morton, p 13, Impact Photos/Steward Weir, p. 20; John T. Hopf, p.25; Juliette Soester, pp. 5, 18, 30, 34, 36; Peter Osborne, p. 29; Photoedit, pp. 19, 35, 43; The Stock Market, pp.17, 21; Topham Picturepoint, p. 11; Zev Radovan, pp 4, 6, 14, 26b, 27, 31, 32.

Cover photograph reproduced with permission of AKG.

Our thanks to Rabbi Allen Secher and Betsey Katz for their comments in the preparation of this book.

Every effort has been made to contact copyright holders of any material reproduced in this book.
Any omissions will be rectified in subsequent printings if notice is given to the Publisher.

Some words are shown in bold, **like this.** You can find out what they mean by looking in the glossary.

Contents

A Note about Dates: in this book, dates are followed by the letters B.C.E. (Before the Common Era) or C.E. (Common Era). This is instead of using the older abbreviations B.C. (Before Christ) and A.D. (*Anno Domini*, meaning "in the year of our Lord"). The date numbers are the same in both systems.

Introducing Judaism

Judaism is one of the oldest religions in the world. It involves beliefs and ways of life that have been important to its followers for more than 4,000 years.

Generally, a Jew is a person whose mother is Jewish or who has converted to Judaism. The branch of Judaism known as **Reform** Judaism also accepts as Jews children born to a non-Jewish mother and a Jewish father. Not everyone who is born Jewish follows the religion. Not all Jews who do follow the religion follow it in the same way. However, most Jews feel that their background and what they share with other Jews is very important.

One way of describing this is to say that Jews think of themselves as being like a large family. In any family, different members may have different opinions and work in different ways, but the fact that they are a family is something that affects them all their lives. Today, Jews live in many different parts of the world, but most Jews feel that they have something in common with other Jews. This is true even if they live far away and in countries where everyday life is quite different.

▲ This Jewish family lives in Jerusalem.

What are Jewish beliefs?

Jews believe that there is one God. They believe that this God is a spirit who is **eternal.** This means he was never born and will never die. He has always existed and always will exist. They believe that he made the world and everything in it, and he loves and cares about what he made. He is so holy that his name cannot be used, but Jews usually call him **Adonai,** which means "Lord." Jews use any name of God with great respect and would never use it carelessly or as a swear word. Many Jews avoid even writing the word *God*. This is why in some Jewish books you sometimes see it written "G-d."

The Covenant

Jews believe that they have a special relationship with God. They are often called the Chosen People. This is because of the **Covenant** that God made with the Jews. A covenant is a solemn agreement. This agreement was that Jews would follow the laws that God gave. In return, he would look after them. The fact that they believe they are the Chosen People does not mean that Jews expect an easy life. It means that they believe they have a greater duty and responsibility to worship God and to live in the right way. They believe that God loves human beings and it is the duty of human beings to love God in return. They believe that this love can be shown by following the instructions that God gave to people about how to live and by worshiping him. Jews believe that these instructions are collected together in the **Torah.** Torah means "Books of Teaching." Jews believe that the Torah is very important.

▼ *Young Jews gather outside a London synagogue.*

Judaism fact check

- Judaism began about 4,000 years ago.
- Jews worship one God whom they often call Adonai.
- The Jewish place of worship is called a synagogue.
- The most important Jewish holy books are called the Torah, which are usually written on scrolls for use in the synagogue or in books for the home and schools.
- The Torah is written in **Hebrew.** Modern Hebrew is the new official language of Israel.
- There are two symbols most often used for Judaism. One is a six-pointed star, called the Star of David or the Magen David (Shield of David). The other symbol is a candlestick with eight branches called a **menorah.**
- There are just over 13 million Jews in the world today.
  - ◆ About 5.8 million Jews live in the United States.
  - ◆ About 4.8 million Jews live in Israel.
  - ◆ About 1.2 million Jews live in Europe.
  - ◆ About 550,000 Jews live in Russia.
  - ◆ There are small Jewish populations in many other countries, including about 100,000 in Australia and 120,000 in Africa.

Abraham and Moses

Judaism began so long ago that no one really knows how it began. Jews believe that two men were most important in shaping the religion and working out the early beliefs. The first of these men was named Abram, later called Abraham. The second was Moses.

Abraham

Jews call Abraham *Avraham Avinu*, which in **Hebrew** means "our father Abraham." He lived about 4,000 years ago in a city called Ur, in modern Iraq. Today, the site of the city has been excavated by archaeologists and is called Tall al Maqayyar. In the days of Abraham, Ur was an important city on the banks of the Euphrates River. It was especially important as a center of worship for the moon god Nanna.

You can find the places mentioned in this book on the map on page 44.

The stories about Abraham were passed down from father to son for hundreds of years before they were written down. This means that we cannot be sure of the details about his life. However, it seems that Abraham was rich and respected, but that he found there were things in his life that did not make him happy. The worship of the moon god and other statues worried him greatly. He seems to have been the first person to act on a belief that there was a greater God who should be worshiped. Guided by his feelings about this God, Abraham and his family left Ur and set out on a journey that he felt was led by the God he worshiped.

Many people who lived in this part of the world were, and still are, nomads. Nomads do not have a fixed home but live in tents. They move these from place to place, usually depending on where their animals can find water in the desert. From this point of view, Abraham's journey was not so unusual. Jews believe that what made it different was that Abraham believed that God was guiding and looking after him.

▲ *Abraham and his family traveled from Ur to Canaan through areas that must have looked similar to this picture of Mount Sinai today.*

Moses

Jews call Moses *Moshe Rabbenu*, which means "our teacher Moses." He lived about 500 years after the time of Abraham. At that time, Jews had been slaves in Egypt for many years and were being treated very badly. Moses came to believe that God wanted him to rescue the Jews. He went to see the **Pharaoh** and told him that if the Jews were not freed, disasters would happen. The Pharaoh did not want to lose the slaves who were working for him, so he refused.

The ten plagues

According to the Jewish holy books, ten disasters called plagues then hit the country. Rivers turned to blood, and there were plagues of frogs, lice, and flies. All the farm animals died, then all the people developed boils. The seventh plague was hailstorms, and this was followed by a plague of locusts. Then there was darkness, and the sun did not shine. The last plague was the death of the eldest son in every Egyptian family. Today, many people would believe that these were natural disasters, but everyone involved then believed that the plagues had been sent by God as a punishment. After the death of the firstborn sons, the Pharaoh allowed the Jews to leave. They were led by Moses to the country of Canaan, which includes the area that today we call Israel.

▲ *Most synagogues have the first words of each of the Ten Commandments on a plaque above the* **ark.**

The Ten Commandments

A commandment is an important rule. Jews believe that the Ten Commandments were given to Moses by God. They are the basis of the Jewish religion and include basic laws that are followed by almost all human beings. They can be summed up like this:

1 I am the Lord your God. You must not have any other gods but me.

2 You must not make any **idols** to worship.

3 You must not use God's name carelessly.

4 You must remember to keep the **Sabbath** day holy.

5 You must respect your father and your mother.

6 You must not murder.

7 You must not commit **adultery.**

8 You must not steal.

9 You must not tell lies about other people.

10 You must not **covet,** or be jealous of that which belongs to another.

Jewish History—The Early Days

Mediterranean Sea

ASHER

NAPHTALI

ZEBULUN

Sea of Galilee

ISSACHAR

N

MANASSEH

Jordan River

EPHRAIM

GAD

DAN

BENJAMIN

JUDAH

Dead Sea

REUBEN

SIMEON

0   50 km

0   50 mi.

▲ This map shows how the land was divided among the Twelve Tribes of Israel.

The beginning

Jewish history is found mainly in the Jewish holy books, written over hundreds of years. The writers' main interest was the relationship between God and the Jewish people, so the books are not like a modern history book. This is the story of the Jewish people as it is found in their holy books. In the early days, the Jews were called **Israelites.**

Jews believe that God led Abraham to a country that he gave to Abraham and his descendants forever. This country was on the shores of the Mediterranean Sea and included the area that today we call Israel. Abraham's family lived there until the time of his grandson, Jacob, when a severe famine hit the area. In order to find food, they went to Egypt, where they settled. Some years later, there was a revolution in Egypt, and a new **Pharaoh** came to the throne. He felt that there was a danger in having a large number of foreigners following their own way of life within his country. So he made them into slaves. Several generations of Israelites lived like this, until the time of Moses, who rescued them. These are the events that Jews remember at the festival of Passover. The Israelites then became nomads in the desert for about 40 years, until they reached the country of Canaan. Moses died when they were within sight of the country. The new leader, Joshua, led the people in.

Judges

Other tribes were settled in Canaan. The Israelites had several years of war before they gained control. Then the land was divided among twelve groups, who are known as the Twelve Tribes of Israel. Each tribe had an area of land of its own. The most important leaders of these tribes were called **Judges.** When there was a problem—usually an enemy attacking one tribe—the Judges could call on other Judges to bring members of their tribe to help. However, it was difficult for the Israelites to be united. The last Judge was a great man called Samuel. The Israelites asked Samuel to choose a king for them, who could rule over all the Israelites and so make them stronger in battle. Samuel chose a man named Saul.

Kings

Saul was king for about 40 years before he was killed in battle. The next king was David. He is probably best remembered for the story about how, as a young boy, he fought a giant named Goliath. Although he was very young, he outwitted the giant and killed him with a stone from his sling. As king, David was very successful. Many Jews still look back to the days of King David as the best time in their history. When he died, his son, Solomon, took over. The country was peaceful and rich. A magnificent new **Temple** was built so that God could be worshiped in a suitable way.

Israel and Judah

After the death of Solomon, the country divided. The northern tribes broke away to make a separate country called Israel. The southern tribes formed the country of Judah. The people who lived there became known as the Jews.

After about 200 years, in 722 B.C.E., Israel was conquered by the Assyrians, who were a great power at the time. Many of the people were taken away to live in Assyria. About 100 years later, in 586 B.C.E., soldiers from Babylon took over the southern kingdom of Judah. Many of the people were taken to live in Babylon. When Cyrus the Great of Persia conquered Babylon in 538 B.C.E., he allowed all the people who had been taken there by the Babylonians to return to their home country if they wished. Some Jews chose to return to Judah, but most chose to stay in Babylon.

▼ *This is a reconstruction of the Ishtar Gate—the main entrance into Babylon at the time the Jews lived there.*

The Diaspora

The **Diaspora** is the name given to Jews living in countries other than Israel. It comes from a word that means "dispersed" or "scattered." The Diaspora began around the time that the Babylonians invaded Judah. Apart from the Jews who were made to leave their country to live in Babylon, other Jews chose to go and live in other countries rather than be ruled by an enemy. This has happened many times in the Jews' history. This is one reason why today there are Jews living in many countries of the world.

Recent Jewish History

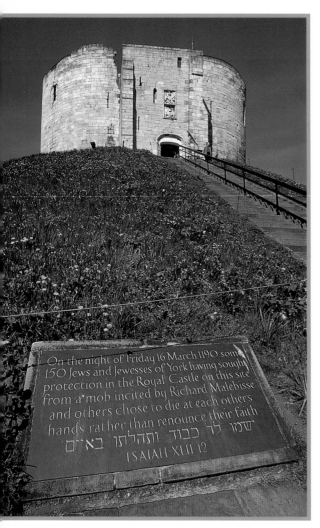

▲ *In the Middle Ages, life was difficult for Jews. In 1190, 150 Jews died in this castle in York, England.*

The plaque reads:

On the night of Friday 16 March 1190 some 150 Jews and Jewesses of York having sought protection in the Royal Castle on this site from a mob incited by Richard Malebisse and others chose to die at each others hands rather than renounce their faith

שמו לו כבוד ותהלתו באיים

ISAIAH XLII 12

Background

For much of their history, Jews have had to fight to keep their identity. Rulers took over their country and put pressure on them to give up their Jewish ways. The Romans took over their country (then called Palestine) in 66 B.C.E. One hundred years later, the Romans crushed a revolt by a group of Jews. As part of this, in 70 C.E., the **Temple**—the most important place of worship for Jews—was destroyed. This was a very important event in Jewish history. Jews today still pray that one day the Temple will be rebuilt. The one wall that remains is a very important site for Jews to visit.

After this revolt, many Jews left Palestine and joined other Jews who were part of the **Diaspora.** For hundreds of years, many Jews led rich lives in many different countries. For others, however, life was difficult. Jews were banned from living in many countries. In other countries, they were forced to live in ghettos— areas of a town that were often walled so that the Jews could be locked in at night. They were treated as if they were not as good as other people. Christians said that Jews were responsible for killing Jesus. In countries that were mainly Christian, Jews were persecuted because of this. Lie!

The Holocaust

In the early years of the twentieth century, there were economic problems in many countries. Germany suffered particular problems because of the crippling conditions that were placed on it at the end of World War I. When the **Nazis** came to power, they wanted to make Germany a great and powerful country again. It was convenient to find a group to blame for the problems. The Nazi leader, Adolf Hitler, hated Jews and began a campaign to get rid of them. First, all Jews had to register. Then they had to wear a yellow Star of David on their clothes so they could be easily identified. Gradually, all their rights were taken away. They were not allowed to own cars, their businesses had to close, their children were not allowed to go to school. Life became harder and harder.

Then the Nazis decided they had found what they called the "final solution to the Jewish problem." This was to get rid of all Jews in the world. Jews were rounded up and sent to special **concentration camps.** Many were killed immediately. Others were starved, beaten, and tortured. By the end of World War II, six million Jews were dead—one-and-a-half-million of them children. One in three of the world's Jewish population had been killed. This time of terrible persecution became known as the **Holocaust.**

After the war

The state of Israel was established in 1948. Its law states that any Jew has the right to live in Israel if they wish to. Almost immediately after it had been established, Israel was at war with its neighbors, because Arabs who were living in the area that had been given to Jews did not want the state of Israel to exist. During the next 50 years, there were several wars between Jews and Arabs, and bombings and terrorist attacks were frequent. In the last years of the twentieth century, changing attitudes and several interventions by successive U.S. presidents led to some improvements in relations. Israel signed peace treaties with Egypt (1979) and Jordan (1994).

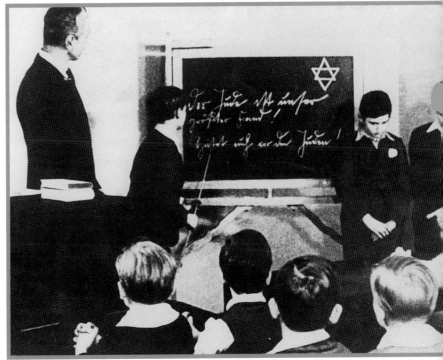

▲ *This picture shows life in Nazi Germany. Two Jewish boys stand at the front, while the class reads from the blackboard "The Jew is our greatest enemy. Beware of the Jew!"*

Anne Frank

Anne Frank was the daughter of a Jewish family living in Holland when it was taken over by the Germans in 1940. In July 1942, the family went into hiding and for more than two years lived in a "Secret Annexe" behind the warehouse that her father had owned. In August 1944, they were betrayed and caught. They were taken to concentration camps and Anne, her sister, and her mother all died. During their time in the Secret Annexe, Anne kept a diary. When they were taken away, the diary was rescued. After the war ended, it was published by Anne's father. It has become a best-seller all over the world. The house where they lived is now a museum, and the Anne Frank House and other charities work to try to educate people toward the end of racism and persecution.

The Different Groups of Jews

▲ *An Orthodox Jew is dressed in traditional clothing for worship.*

In any religion, different individuals have different opinions. The followers of Judaism do not agree about everything. They are all individuals, and what is very important to one may be less important to another. They all share the most important beliefs, although the way in which those beliefs affect their lives is not the same for everyone. In Europe, there are two main groups of Jews today. These are **Orthodox** Jews and Progressive Jews. In North America, the main groups of Jews today are Orthodox Jews, **Reform** Jews, **Conservative** Jews, and Reconstructionist Jews.

Orthodox Jews

Orthodox Jews believe that the **Torah** is the word of God. They believe that it teaches how God wants people to live and that it will never change. They believe that the teaching stays the same, even though at different times it will be applied in different ways. This means that no matter when or where they live, people will always know what God wants for them.

Both at home and in the synagogue, Orthodox Jews are more likely to follow strictly all the laws of the Torah. In the synagogue, men and women sit separately, and women do not take part in leading the service. At weekday morning services, men wear the traditional **tefillin** as well as the **yarmulka,** or skullcap, and prayer robe that most Jewish men wear.

The **Hasidic** movement is one of the most important groups of Orthodox Jews. It began in Poland in the seventeenth century. Today, there are Hasidic communities in many cities, including Jerusalem, London, Chicago, New York, and Melbourne. They emphasize trusting in God, reading the holy books, and observing the **Sabbath.** They have their own schools and synagogues, and many Hasidic Jews still wear traditional Polish clothes. The men wear beards and sidelocks and dress in black. They keep their heads covered at all times. The women dress modestly with long skirts and long sleeves.

Reform Jews and Conservative Jews

Reform Jews and Conservative Jews share the belief that Judaism can change to suit different circumstances.

The Reform movement began in Germany in the nineteenth century. It teaches that it is not necessary to obey all the laws of the Torah and that laws can be changed or ignored if they are no longer appropriate. Generally, the changes make it easier for Jews to live among people who do not share their religion. Today, Reform Jews believe that moral and ethical teachings form the most important part of Judaism. Many feel that traditional practices have no meaning for them. However, they are increasingly returning to traditional practices.

Conservative Judaism also began in the nineteenth century. Conservative Jews consider a collection of writings called the **Talmud** to be as much an authority as the Bible. However, they believe that Jewish practice may be changed to fit the times. They believe this helps make Judaism relevant for each generation.

▲ *In Reform Judaism, women can become Rabbis.*

Orthodox Jews	Reform and Conservative Jews
In the synagogue	
• Men always wear special clothes for worship	• Men may wear a skullcap, but do not usually wear special clothes
• Women sit in a separate gallery	• Men and women sit together
• Men always lead the worship; only men may become **rabbis**	• Men and women lead worship; women can become rabbis
• Services always use the **Hebrew** language	• Services usually held in everyday language
• **Bar mitzvah** held for boys at 13; different observance for girls	• Same services held for boys and girls at 13
Orthodox and Conservative Jews	**Reform and Liberal Jews**
At home	
• Sabbath is kept as a day of total rest	• Sabbath is a day not to attend paid work
• Rules about **kosher** food kept strictly	• Rules about kosher food may not be strictly observed
• Festivals follow the traditional observances	• Some **fasts** are not observed, Sabbath and festivals do not always begin at sunset
• Someone is counted as Jewish only if their mother was	• Someone is Jewish if either parent was, or if they were brought up as a Jew

Jewish Holy Books

Jews are sometimes called the People of the Book. Their holy books are very important to their life and their religion. The complete Scriptures are called the **Tenakh.** They are divided into three sections. The first is the **Torah,** the Books of Teaching. The second is the **Nevi'im,** the Books of the Prophets. The third is the **Ketuvim,** the Books of Writings. Putting the first letters of these three Hebrew words together—T, N, K—gives the word *Tenakh*.

The Torah

The five books of the Torah are **Genesis, Exodus, Leviticus, Numbers,** and **Deuteronomy.** They are sometimes known as the Five Books of Moses. The books are the history of the beginning of the Jewish people. Jews believe that they contain instructions about how God wants them to live. Jews call these instructions **mitzvot,** which means "commandments." Jewish tradition says that there are 613 mitzvot. Of those, 248 mitzvot are things that Jews are commanded to do, such as honoring parents and keeping the **Sabbath.** The other 365 mitzvot are things that Jews are commanded not to do, such as stealing and murdering. Some Jews strictly keep the mitzvot.

Sefer Torah

▼ *This is an open scroll of the Torah, showing how it is wound onto rollers.*

The Torah is written in columns on scrolls, so it can be read in the synagogue. A scroll is like a book with one long page wound around two wooden rollers, one at each end. A full-size scroll is about 197 feet (60 meters) long unwound. A scroll of the Torah is called a **Sefer Torah.** Each copy is written by hand by a specially trained scribe. The scribe uses special ink and a quill pen. A Sefer Torah takes more than a year to complete.

The material used for a scroll is **parchment,** not paper. Parchment is animal skin that has been specially treated and smoothed so that it can be written on. Many scrolls used in synagogues are very old and valuable. All scrolls are treated with great care, and the parchment is never touched by hands. A special pointer called a **yad** is used to follow the words as the scroll is read in the synagogue. If the text were to become smudged or damaged, the scroll could not be used.

The Nevi'im

The Nevi'im is a collection of history books. It includes the teachings of the **prophets.** All through Jewish history there have been men and women who felt that they were inspired by God to give messages to the Jews. Sometimes their messages grew out of a particular situation, but Jews believe that much of what they taught still has meaning today. Three of the most important prophets were Elijah, Isaiah, and Jeremiah, but there are many others.

Some parts of the books of the Nevi'im are read in services in the synagogue. They are not usually written on scrolls. Others are not read in services, but Jews may read and study them at home.

The Ketuvim

Ketuvim means "writings," and the Ketuvim includes many different types of writing. Many of the books are stories from the history of the Jews. A book that is used frequently in the synagogue and at home is the Book of **Psalms.** A psalm is a type of poem. It can be used like a religious song. Many of the Psalms are supposed to have been written by King David. Some of the other books of the Ketuvim are read at particular festivals.

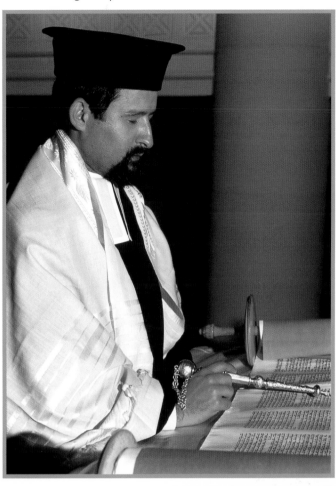

▼ *A rabbi reads the Torah in the synagogue, using the yad to follow the words.*

Other writings

In addition to the Tenakh, there are other writings of great importance to Jews. For hundreds of years, the leaders of Judaism handed down oral (spoken) traditions about the mitzvot, explaining how they were to be kept.

By 200 C.E., Jews were dispersing around the Roman Empire because of ill treatment. A Jewish leader and **rabbi** at this time saw that it was necessary to write down the oral traditions so that different Jewish groups did not grow apart. This written record was called the **Mishnah.** The Mishnah was studied by Jews, especially in Israel and Babylon, and their discussions about it were carefully written down. About 500 C.E., these discussions were collected together and organized. Each paragraph of the Mishnah was written down, with the discussions and comments next to it. This collection is called the **Talmud.** The Talmud is very important for Jews today. It still is studied carefully by Jewish scholars and is the basis of observance, more so than the Tenakh.

What the Holy Books Say

The holy books of Judaism contain thousands of years of history, stories, rules, and instructions. They have been known and loved by Jews for more than 4,000 years. Here are some "snapshots" of what they contain.

The creation

The book of **Genesis** begins with the story of the creation of the world. It says that for six days, God commanded things to happen. These commands brought the world as we know it into being.

God commanded:

Day 1: light
Day 2: Earth's atmosphere ("a dome over the Earth")
Day 3: the land to divide from the sea, and plants to grow on the land
Day 4: sun, moon, and stars, and so day and night, years, and seasons
Day 5: sea creatures and birds
Day 6: land animals and human beings.

On the seventh day, God rested because creation was finished and *"he saw that it was good."* It is because of this that Jews rest on the seventh day, Saturday, which they call the **Sabbath.**

▲ *This scribe is writing on a* **mezuzah** *scroll with a special quill pen. A mezuzah contains the first two paragraphs of the Sh'ma.*

The Sh'ma

The Sh'ma is the most important Jewish prayer. Jews say the Sh'ma when they get up in the morning and before they go to bed at night. It is recited as part of the morning and evening services in the synagogue. It also is said by a Jew who is dying, if he or she is able to speak. If not, it is repeated by the relatives at the bedside. This is what the Sh'ma says:

Hear, Israel, the Lord is our God, the Lord is one. Now you must love the Lord your God with all your heart, and with all your soul and with all your strength. And these words, which I am commanding you today, shall be upon your heart. And you shall teach them carefully to your children, and speak of them when you are sitting in your house, when you are walking along the road, when you lie down, and when you rise up. And you must bind them as a sign upon your arm, and they shall be a token between your eyes. And you must write them on the doorposts of your house and on your gates. (**Deuteronomy** 6:4–9)

The Prophets

There are 21 Books of **Prophets** in the **Nevi'im.** Stories and teaching from other prophets also are found in the **Torah.** Some of the books are very long. For example, the Book of Isaiah has 60 chapters. Others are very short and contain only a few chapters. Here are a few examples of what the prophets say:

No longer shall you need the sun for light by day, nor the shining of the moon by night, for the Lord shall be your light everlasting, your God shall be your glory. Your sun shall set no more, your moon no more withdraw, for the Lord shall be a light to you forever and your days of mourning shall be ended. (Isaiah 60:19–20)

This is what the Lord asks of you: only to do justice and to love mercy and to walk humbly with your God. (Micah 6:8)

The word of the Lord came to me, as follows, 'Before I formed you in the womb, I knew you, and before you were born I made you holy —I have appointed you to be a prophet to the nations.' But I said, 'But, Lord God, look, I do not know how to speak, for I am still young.' Then the Lord said to me, 'Do not say "I am still young," for everywhere I will send you, you will go, and everything I command you, you will speak. Do not be afraid, for I am with you to take care of you.' (Jeremiah 1:4-8)

They shall beat their swords into ploughshares and their spears into pruning hooks. Nation shall not lift up sword against nation, nor shall they practice for war anymore. (Isaiah 2:4)

These words of peace from Isaiah 2: 4 were thought to be so fitting that they are carved on the wall of the United Nations Building in New York. The United Nations is an international organization formed in 1945 to try to encourage countries to work peacefully together.

▼ *The United Nations Building in New York contains words of peace from Isaiah 2:4.*

Worship at Home

The way in which Jews live is an important part of their belief. They believe that life itself was given by God. So even ordinary everyday things such as preparing a meal or going to bed should include God and are ways in which Jews can worship Him.

▲ *A mezuzah is always attached to the right-hand doorpost.*

Mezuzah

The **mezuzah** is a tiny scroll made of **parchment.** On it are written the first two paragraphs of the Sh'ma, the most important Jewish prayer. This scroll is usually covered with a special case made of wood, plastic, or metal then attached to the right-hand side of the doorpost. Mezuzahs can be attached to the doorway of every room except those of the bathroom, which is not thought a suitable place for a holy object. Jews touch the mezuzah on their way in and out of the room. This is a way of reminding themselves that God is always there. It also reminds them of God's promise that "you are blessed when you come in and blessed when you go out" (**Deuteronomy** 28:6).

Daily worship

Jews may pray at any time. There are special prayers for getting up in the morning and before going to bed and before and after meals. They show that God is at the center of Jews' lives. Jewish men wear the **yarmulka,** a skullcap, for synagogue worship. Some men wear it all the time. Covering the head like this is a sign of the person's respect for God. In some **Reform** synagogues, women also wear the yarmulka. **Orthodox** Jewish men also wear a **tallit katan** under their clothes. A tallit katan is rectangular, usually made of wool, and worn over the shoulders. It has fringes at each end. This is different from the much larger tallit, properly called a **tallit gadol,** which Jewish men wear for some services in the synagogue.

Sabbath in the home

Sabbath—in **Hebrew** Shabbat—is the Jewish day of rest and worship. It begins at sunset on Friday and lasts until sunset on Saturday. All Jewish days are counted from sunset to sunset because in **Genesis** it says, "Evening passed and morning came—that was the first day" (Genesis 1:5). On Friday, the house is cleaned and tidied and the Sabbath eve meal is prepared. The Sabbath begins when the wife or mother of the family lights two candles and says a prayer that welcomes the Sabbath.

After the synagogue service on Friday evening, the family eat the Sabbath eve meal. This is the most important meal of the week and is always the best the family can afford. It always includes two loaves of **challah** bread. The meal offers a chance for the family to be together and is a relaxed and happy occasion.

Keeping the Sabbath

On the Sabbath, Jews remember that in the story of creation, God made the world in six days and rested on the seventh day. So on this day, Jews do no work. For strict Orthodox Jews, this does not just mean their jobs. It means not doing anything that is considered work. This includes cooking—food is prepared the day before. It also includes driving a car, shopping, and so on. It makes the day one in which Jews can relax at home or with friends without rushing around doing chores. The Sabbath ends with the **Havdalah** ceremony. There are prayers, and a special braided candle is lit. Everyone smells a box of spices and hopes that the peace of the Sabbath will spread through the coming week, just as the smell of the spices spreads through the house.

▲ *Lighting the Sabbath candles means that the Sabbath has begun.*

Jonathan's view

Jonathan, 13, comes from an Orthodox Jewish family in England.

I enjoy Shabbat, because it is a special day. Sometimes we call it Queen Shabbat to show how special it is. I always get quite excited on Friday. In winter, school finishes so that we can get home before it is dark. The house is ready, and then Mum lights the candles and says the prayer that means Shabbat has begun. I really like the idea that what we are doing is what Jews have done for thousands of years and are still doing all over the world. It makes me feel a part of a really important tradition. I know some people who aren't Jewish think it must be a very boring day, but it isn't. It's a day for enjoying yourself quietly and getting ready for a busy week.

Worship in the Synagogue

Jews believe that they can worship God anywhere. But like most religions, they have special places for worship. They are called synagogues. Jews do not usually use the word *synagogue*. Many call it **shul** (rhymes with rule). Some use the name Bet ha Knesset, which means "place of meeting." **Reform** Jews call it the **Temple.** Synagogues likely began around the time the Jews had been taken away to Babylon after the destruction of Jerusalem in 586 B.C.E. They began meeting in houses so they could pray and study together. Then special buildings were set aside for Jews to meet for worship and study.

When some Jews enter a synagogue they wash their hands. This is to make them feel cleansed to worship God. Then they say a prayer that thanks God that they can worship Him. Part of the prayer says:

> *I will worship facing toward your holy Temple. Lord, I love the dwelling of your house and the place where your glory rests. I will worship and bow and bend my knee before the Lord my maker.*

A full **Orthodox** synagogue service cannot take place unless there is a **minyan**—a group of ten adult men. If there are fewer than ten men, the service can still go on, but some prayers are omitted. Women are counted as part of the minyan in Reform and most **Conservative** synagogues.

▼ *Orthodox Jewish men wear special clothes at most services.*

Special clothes

In Orthodox and Conservative synagogues, men wear special clothes for worship. They wear the **yarmulka,** which some Jewish men wear all the time. They also wear a special shawl, called a tallit, over their clothes. This is usually rectangular and made of wool or silk. It has a fringe and tassels at each end. These are there because the **Torah** tells Jews to put tassels on their clothes to help them remember God's commandments (**Numbers** 15:39). In some Reform synagogues, women also can wear the yarmulka and tallit.

For weekday services in Orthodox synagogues, men also wear two small leather boxes. These are called **tefillin.** They contain small pieces of **parchment** that have the first two paragraphs of the Sh'ma written on them. The boxes have long straps attached to them. If the person is right-handed, one box is worn on the upper part of the left arm. It is placed so that when the arm is resting, the box points toward the heart. This reminds Jews that it is important to love God. The other box is worn so that it is in the center of the forehead, just above where the hair starts to grow. This reminds Jews that they must love and serve God with their mind. Orthodox Jewish men may wear tefillin for prayers at home, too.

▲ *A rabbi inspects the scroll from a tefillah.*

Caring for tefillin

Like **mezuzah,** tefillin are very important objects for Jews. Both mezuzahs and tefillin can be written only by a trained scribe using special materials. They must be opened and checked by a **rabbi** about once every three years to make sure that the writing has not faded. If it is undamaged, the writing can be written over. If the parchment has cracked, it must be replaced. Jews always handle mezuzahs and tefillin with great care and respect.

Rabbis

Rabbi is a **Hebrew** word that means "master" or "teacher"—in other words, a respected leader. Rabbis are the leaders of Jewish communities. They are respected because they have studied the Torah and other Scriptures and know a great deal about Jewish law. In the synagogue, the rabbi often leads the prayers and may give an address during the service. A rabbi also conducts services such as weddings and funerals. Many rabbis lead classes, educating members of the Jewish community about Judaism and helping them learn more about Jewish texts such as the Torah.

Rabbis often are asked to make decisions about Jewish law—for example, about whether or not a particular item of food is **kosher** and therefore fit for Jews to eat. Three rabbis together form a **bet din,** which is a Jewish court. These courts are important in deciding matters of Jewish law and also issue the **get,** the certificate of Jewish divorce. It is a bet din that organizes matters when a person wishes to **convert** to Judaism. In the Jewish community, rabbis often are asked for their advice because they are so respected by the people. Some are marriage guidance counselors. Others are chaplains to hospitals or prisons so that they can help look after any Jews who are there.

Synagogues

Like any building, synagogues reflect the time when they were built and the attitudes and amount of money available to the people who built them. The way that a synagogue is designed and the things that are in it, are reminders of the **Temple** in Jerusalem. The architectural style of a synagogue generally follows the culture of the place where it was built. Whatever they look like, most synagogues have a Star of David outside and there is usually **Hebrew** writing above the doorway. Inside, all synagogues are almost always built on a similar pattern.

The ark

At the front of the synagogue is a special cupboard or alcove called the holy **ark.** This is where the scrolls are kept when they are not being read. The scrolls are the most holy objects in the synagogue, and they are treated with great care. When the scroll is not being read, it is wrapped in a special cover sometimes called a **mantle.** These are often made of silk or velvet. However, in some branches of Judaism, covers are made of wood covered with silk. They are beautifully decorated. Covers are sometimes presented to the synagogue by someone wishing to celebrate a special event in their life or to remember a relative who has died. The scrolls also are decorated with metal crowns and bells attached to the end of the wooden rollers. These also are to remind people that the scrolls are special. Next to the ark are special seats for the **rabbi** and **cantor,** who lead the worship in the synagogue. There may be similar seats that can be used by visiting speakers or synagogue officers.

◀ *Scrolls and their mantles are stored in the ark, a special cupboard, when they are not being read.*

Ner Tamid

Above the ark is the **ner tamid.** This means "continual light." It is a light that never goes out. It is a reminder that God is always present. It is also a reminder of the lamp that burned in the Temple and never went out.

Women's area

In some synagogues, it is not considered right for men and women to sit together. Women and young children sit in one area, while men sit in another. The women's area may be a gallery upstairs or a separate section at the back or side. In other synagogues, everyone sits together.

Other areas

Ever since synagogues began, they have been used for other things in addition to worship. In earlier centuries, they often had rooms where Jews who were on a journey could stay. Today, there is usually a hall that can be used by members of the synagogue for wedding receptions or **bar** and **bat mitzvah** parties. It also may be used by the youth club, senior citizens group, or any other group that the synagogue runs. In addition, there are almost always school classrooms that can be used for teaching Hebrew and Jewish subjects to children.

▼ **Orthodox** *Jewish teenagers attend a summer camp in upstate New York.*

David's view

David, 15, lives in New York.

I enjoy going to Temple. Sometimes I go to the morning service with my father before he goes to work and I go to school. I know he finds it really helpful. He says that it's good to pray before you go off to work and to all the worries and stresses that a normal day brings. As well as the importance of the worship, I must admit that I still enjoy the feeling that I'm counted as a man. That's only happened since my bar mitzvah earlier this year. I like the festival services best, especially Simhat Torah, when we are given candy at the end of the service! It's good that some of my friends from school go to the same Temple. It means we know a lot of the same people and helps make us better buddies.

Major Places of Worship

The First Temple

The First **Temple** in Jerusalem was the most important place for Jews to worship God. It was the center of their religion. For hundreds of years, Jews believed that it was the only place where they could worship God fully.

You can find the places mentioned in this book on the map on page 44.

The First Temple was built by King Solomon in about 960 B.C.E. It took seven years to build and was magnificent. The Book of Chronicles describes Solomon's plans to build a Temple fit to worship God:

> I am building a Temple to honor the Lord my God. It will be a holy place where my people and I will worship him by burning incense of fragrant spices . . . Send me a man with skill in engraving, in working gold, silver, bronze, and iron, and in making blue, purple, and red cloth. (2 Chronicles 2:4 and 7)

This Temple was destroyed when the Babylonians conquered the Jews' country in 586 B.C.E.

The Second Temple

When Jews returned to Jerusalem, the Second Temple was built on the same site. Jews came from all over the world to worship there. They made sacrifices and listened to the **Torah** being read. The Second Temple was busiest on Mondays and Thursdays, which were market days in Jerusalem.

▼ After they had destroyed the Second Temple in 70 C.E., the Romans took its treasures to Rome, as shown in this relief from the Arch of Titus.

The custom began of reading the Torah scrolls then as well as on Saturdays—the **Sabbath.** Today, the Torah is still read in synagogues on these days.

When Herod the Great became king in 39 B.C.E., he began rebuilding the Temple and made it one of the most splendid buildings in the world. The outer walls were made of marble. Anyone could go into the outer courtyard, but only Jews were allowed into the second area. Only priests were allowed into the center courtyard, where the Temple lamp was kept burning.

During the first century B.C.E., Palestine became part of the Roman Empire. In 66 C.E., the Jews rebelled against Rome. The Romans crushed the rebellion. They entered the Temple and destroyed it. The whole place was burned and the Temple treasures were taken to Rome. The anniversary of the day on which the Temple was burned is a day of **fasting** for Jews, and is the saddest day of the Jewish year.

Orthodox and **Conservative** Jews still pray every day that the Temple will be restored. The only part of the Temple that survives is the Western Wall.

Keeping the memory of the Temple alive

Orthodox Jews hope and pray every day that one day the Temple will be restored. In the synagogue, prayers take place at the time sacrifices were offered in the Temple each day and they always mention the Temple. At festivals, the readings from the Torah describe the Temple sacrifices offered at that festival. Whenever Orthodox Jews eat bread, they dip the first piece lightly in salt to remember the salt that was sprinkled on the sacrifices. At the end of a traditional Jewish wedding service, the groom breaks a glass under his foot to remind Jews that their joy can never be complete until the Temple is rebuilt.

The Touro synagogue

The Touro synagogue in Newport, Rhode Island, is the oldest synagogue in the United States. It was built in 1759. Many people believe that it is one of the best examples of eighteenth-century architecture in America.

The synagogue was built of brick that was imported from England. It stands at an acute angle to the street, so that the **ark** can face Jerusalem and the site of the Temple. The women's gallery is supported by twelve columns to remember the twelve tribes of Israel. Each one was made from a solid tree trunk. The congregation that began the synagogue had traveled to America to escape persecution in Europe, so there is a trapdoor under the reading desk. This shows that even when the synagogue was built, they were still afraid of attack.

Today, the synagogue is a well-used place of worship. It is visited by more than 25,000 people every year.

▶ *America's oldest synagogue, the Touro synagogue, is in Newport, Rhode Island.*

Pilgrimage

A **pilgrimage** is a journey that people make because of their religion. It may involve going to the place where the religion began or to somewhere that is important in its history. In the days of **Temple** worship, men were expected to make a pilgrimage to Jerusalem for the major festivals. Today, these festivals are celebrated at home, and Judaism does not require its followers to go on pilgrimages. However, Israel is a very important country for Jews. Many who do not live there aim to travel there not as tourists but as pilgrims.

You can find the places mentioned in this book on the map on page 44.

The Western Wall

The most important place of pilgrimage for Jews is in Jerusalem. It is called the Western Wall. It is all that remains of the Second Temple. Jews go there to pray and to grieve for the loss of the Temple. They may carefully place small pieces of paper with prayers written on them into the spaces between the stones. Men and women pray separately. The sound of the prayers is the reason why non-Jews used to call the wall the "Wailing Wall."

▼ *Prayers are carefully placed in the gaps in the Wall.*

Between the war that immediately followed the establishment of the state of Israel in 1948 and the Six-Day War in 1967, Jerusalem was divided in two. Jews lived in the west; Arabs lived in the east, which included the old walled city. This meant that no Jews could visit the remains of the Temple. As a result of the Six-Day War, Jews took control of the old city. Since that time daily services have been held at the Western Wall. The rest of the Temple site is occupied by a Muslim mosque, the Mosque of the Dome of the Rock.

▲ *The Western Wall is all that remains of the Temple built by Herod in 39 B.C.E., which was destroyed by the Romans in 70 C.E..*

Yad Vashem

Another important place of pilgrimage for Jews is Yad Vashem. This is also in Jerusalem. It covers 45 acres in an area called the Mount of Remembrance. Yad Vashem was set up in 1953. It is a combination of a shrine and exhibitions that are a memorial to the six million Jews who died in the **Holocaust.** Many Jews today remember family members who were killed during World War II.

Yad Vashem has the largest library of information about the Holocaust in the world, with more than 50 million pages of documents. It also holds hundreds of thousands of photographs and films. Some of these form part of the exhibitions. There are photographs of the **concentration camps** and the Jews who were imprisoned in them. There are displays of their clothing and other possessions.

Yad Vashem is made up of several different shrines, each intended to show a different aspect of the horror of the Holocaust. The Hall of Remembrance is a darkened room something like a tent. It has a huge map. The names of death camps are engraved in **Hebrew** and English, and candles burn all the time to mark each one.

Part of the site is a Garden of the Righteous of the Nations, where trees and, more recently, a Wall of Honor commemorate non-Jewish men and women who risked their lives or their safety to rescue Jews. Names are still being added to this list, which in 1999 had more than 16,000 names on it.

In Israel, Nisan 27th in the seventh month of the Jewish year is a day of remembrance for Jews who died in the Holocaust. This makes it a special day for people to visit Yad Vashem, although many Jews go there at other times, too.

Monument to a nation's grief

Abba Eban, an important Jewish politician at the time that Yad Vashem was begun, said:

*"Yad Vashem is the monument to a nation's grief. It gives moving testimony to the unparalleled violence that afflicted the Jewish people at the hands of **Nazi** Germany, leaving a vast legacy of death and suffering in its wake. Yad Vashem is therefore one of the most significant landmarks in the moral history of mankind. It merits the reverence and support of free people everywhere."*

▼ *This is a sculpture at Yad Vashem.*

Festivals—Rosh Ha-shanah and Yom Kippur

Rosh Ha-shanah

Rosh Ha-shanah is the Jewish New Year. According to Jewish tradition, it is the anniversary of the beginning of the world—the day when God first

created human beings. On the night before Rosh Ha-shanah, some Jews eat a meal that includes apples dipped in honey. They say to each other, "May it be the Lord's will to renew us for a year that will be good and sweet." In other words, the apples and honey are a way of saying that they hope the coming year will be a pleasant one.

At the synagogue service the following day, Jews offer each other good wishes for the new year. However, the service also has a more serious tone. It is the beginning of the most solemn time of the Jewish year, called the Days of Repentance, or Returning. These are the days when Jews reflect on all the things they have done wrong during the past year. At the synagogue service, Jews ask for forgiveness and promise themselves and God that they will do better in the year to come. During the service, the **shofar** is blown. This is a musical instrument made from a ram's horn. It plays two notes and sounds somewhat like a trumpet—very loud and solemn. The shofar is sounded 100 times. Each time, Jews believe that it is reminding them to be sorry for all the things they have done wrong.

▲ *The shofar is made from a ram's horn.*

In some places, Jewish families meet after lunch on Rosh Ha-shanah and go for a walk. If there is a beach nearby, they will go there, otherwise they walk to a river. They empty crumbs from their pockets and throw them into the water. The way the crumbs are carried away by the water is a symbol of the Jews' hope that their sins will be forgiven.

The Days of Repentance

The Days of Repentance or Returning are the days between Rosh Ha-shanah and Yom Kippur, the **Day of Atonement.** During these ten days, Jews try to put right things that are wrong in their lives. For example, they make sure to settle any arguments they have had and that their life is in order. This is so that at the end of the ten days, they are ready to "return" to God.

▶ *On Yom Kippur some Jews wear white. Some men wear a white robe such as this one over their clothes.*

Yom Kippur

Yom Kippur means "Day of Atonement." Atonement means to make up for something you have done wrong. Jews believe that they can pray to God for forgiveness at any time. However, Yom Kippur is a day set aside to ask God to forgive them for all the things they have done wrong. They can then become "at one" with God. They believe that if they are really sorry for what they have done, and have made things right with other people, God will forgive them. This means that the day is also a time for celebrating God's goodness and how much he loves them.

At Yom Kippur, Jews **fast** for 25 hours. This helps them concentrate on prayers. They spend most of the day at the synagogue. In the synagogue, the **ark** and the reading desk are covered in white cloths. The people leading the service wear white, too. This is a symbol of purity and shows that they believe God will take away their sins. At the end of the Yom Kippur service, the shofar is blown again. Its meaning now is different from when it was blown at Rosh Ha-shanah. This time, it reminds the people of all the good they have promised themselves and God that they will do in the coming year.

The calendar

Jews use the calendar that is used by most people in Western countries, but they also have their own calendar. It has different months and a different numbering system for the years, which go back to the creation following the book of **Genesis.** The years begin in late September or early October and are 3,761 years ahead of the Western calendar. So, for example, autumn 2005 will be the start of the Jewish year 5766, 2010 the start of 5771, and so on. Jewish months start at the new moon and last for 29 or 30 days. Festivals occur on fixed dates in these months. Every three years, an extra month—Veadar— is added to the calendar so that the years keep pace with the "solar years" on which the Western calendar is based.

Hebrew month	Western equivalent
Tishri	September/October
Heshvan	October/November
Kislev	November/December
Tebet	December/January
Shebat	January/February
Adar	February/March
Nisan	March/April
Iyar	April/May
Sivan	May/June
Tammuz	June/July
Ab	July/August
Elul	August/September

Festivals—Pesah

Pesah is the Festival of Passover. It is the most important Jewish festival, and it celebrates events that happened nearly 4,000 years ago. The **Israelites** had been slaves in Egypt for hundreds of years, and Moses became aware that God wanted him to organize their release. The **Pharaoh** refused to let them go because they were doing very useful work. Moses warned him that a series of disasters would hit the country. This came true, and after the tenth of these disasters—the death of the first-born son in every Egyptian house — the Pharaoh said that they could go. The Israelites left immediately. They did not even wait for the bread they had been making for the journey to rise. Although he had said they could leave, the Pharaoh changed his mind soon after they had gone. He sent his soldiers after them. The Israelites were saved when the water in the Red Sea parted to allow them across and then closed again.

Jews remember these events in the festival of Passover every year. It lasts eight days and, for those eight days, Jews do not come into contact with anything that contains leaven. Leaven is anything similar to yeast or self-rising flour that contains a raising agent. The house is searched carefully to make sure there are no crumbs hidden—down the sides of armchairs, for example. Nothing that contains leaven is eaten during the festival. Different containers are used for washing dishes. Different dishes, silverware, and kitchen utensils are used for the festival. This is to make sure there is no trace of leaven anywhere. Strictly **Orthodox** Jews and **Conservative** Jews only eat foods that have been approved as "**kosher** for Passover."

▲ *This family is practicing "Bedikat hametz"— searching for leaven.*

The Seder

The **Seder** is a ceremonial meal and is the main part of the Passover celebrations. The meal follows a special order written down in a book called the Haggadah. The book tells how the Jews were slaves in Egypt and how they escaped. The story is told as the meal is eaten. The youngest person at the meal asks four questions, and the oldest person answers them. The first question is, "Why is this night different from all other nights?" The questions and answers tell the story.

In the center of the table is the Seder plate. It is divided into five sections and has special foods on it. Other things on the table also have a symbolic meaning related to the story:

- A bowl of saltwater is a symbol of the tears that the slaves cried.

- There is a glass of wine for each person. Wine is drunk four times during the meal, as a reminder that God promised four times he would free them.

- **Matzoh** are sheets of unleavened bread similar to flat crackers. They are a reminder of the bread that did not have time to rise before the Jews fled.

- A glass of wine for Elijah, one of the greatest **prophets** of Judaism. Jews believe that one day he will return to announce the coming of the **Messiah.**

The Seder also includes a regular meal. This may be anything that the family wishes to eat. After the meal, they usually stay at the table to complete the Seder and sing songs. The traditional songs often have repeated words and choruses so that even very young children can join in. The meal is a strong link with the Jews' history and looks forward to a time of peace and joy. The last words of the Seder are "Next year in Jerusalem, next year may all be free."

The symbols on the Seder plate

Shank bone of lamb—This is not eaten but serves as a reminder of the lambs sacrificed in Biblical times. The **Israelites** put lambs' blood above their doors so that the Angel of Death passed over them during the tenth plague. This gives the Passover festival its name.

Egg—It is hardboiled, then roasted in a flame as a symbol of new life.

Green vegetable—This is usually parsley or lettuce and is a symbol of the green of springtime.

Bitter herbs—Often horseradish, the herbs are a reminder of the bitterness of slavery.

Charoset—This sweet mixture of nuts, apples, spices, and wine is a reminder of the "cement" used by the slaves when they were building and of the sweetness of freedom.

▲ The Seder plate contains five symbols for Passover.

Festivals—Sukkot

The second festival of the Jewish year is Sukkot, the Feast of **Tabernacles.** A tabernacle is a hut or tent. The **Hebrew** word for this is *sukkah.* As part of their celebrations of the festival, Jews build a sukkah in the garden and live in it for the week that the festival lasts. This is to remind them of the time after the **Israelites** had left Egypt and were traveling in the desert. For 40 years they had no fixed home. They lived in sukkot that they built when they reached an oasis, where they could find water. The other purpose of Sukkot is to be a reminder of the days when Jews used to take offerings of fruit to the **Temple** in Jerusalem.

A sukkah

A sukkah can be any size, but it must be large enough for at least one person to sit in. Sometimes Jews build a sukkah at the synagogue large enough for everyone who worships there to sit in. A sukkah must have at least three walls. The most important part is the roof. It must be made of branches and leaves that are nonedible. It should be large enough to provide shade but not so thick that people cannot see the sky . (For the same reason, a sukkah cannot be built under a tree or where a building hides the sky.) The roof is often decorated with fruit, and the sukkah may have other decorations in it.

▲ *Some Jews build a sukkah for the whole synagogue congregation.*

Sara's view

Sara, 14, lives in Tel Aviv, Israel.

Sukkot is one of my favorite festivals. My brother and I make paper chains and other decorations to put in the sukkah and then we help to decorate it. We usually have little electric lights there, too. We use the garden shed, which has a roof we can lift off so that we can build the sukkah out of it every year. We eat our meals there, and sometimes we are allowed to camp out there at night. It makes it a real adventure. I like the idea that we are living in the same way as our ancestors did thousands of years ago.

The lulav

At the synagogue services on each day of Sukkot except the **Sabbath,**
Jews hold a **lulav.** This is a collection of branches from particular trees—
palm, willow, and myrtle. The branches are tied together and held in the
right hand. In the left hand they hold a citron, a fruit similar to a lemon.
Each of these is a symbol—something that has a deep meaning. The palm
is a symbol of the spine. The willow is a symbol of the lips. The myrtle is
a symbol of the eyes. The citron is a symbol of the heart. Holding the four
things together is a symbol of the Jewish belief that God must be
worshiped with every part of one's being.

During the synagogue services, one man holds a **Torah** scroll. The other
men walk around him holding the lulav. This is a reminder of how, in the
days of the Temple, the people used to circle around the altar. The lulav
also is waved in all six directions and back again toward the man's heart.
This is a symbol that God is the ruler of the universe.

Simhat Torah

The day after the end of Sukkot is called Simhat Torah. This means "the
Rejoicing of the Torah." The books of the Torah are very important for
Jews. Each week, parts of the books are read in the services in the
synagogue. During the year, the five books are read all the way through. At
Simhat Torah, there is a special ceremony in which the very last part of the
Book of **Deuteronomy** is read, followed by the first part of the Book of
Genesis. In this way, the
readings start all over again.

▼ *Jews dance around the synagogue at Simhat Torah.*

Jews believe that the books of
the Torah tell how God wants
them to live. Making sure that
the readings go on without
stopping is the way Jews show
that they should never stop
following what God wants.

Simhat Torah is a joyful
occasion. All the scrolls are
taken from the **ark** and carried
around the synagogue with
the people dancing, singing,
and clapping after them.
Children are given sweets,
chocolate, and fruit as part of
the celebration.

Festivals—Shavuot and Purim

Shavuot and Purim are festivals that celebrate events in Jewish history. Shavuot is a more important festival.

▲ *The synagogue is decorated for Shavuot.*

Shavuot

Shavuot is held seven weeks after Passover, so it is sometimes called the Feast of Weeks. It is the festival that celebrates God giving the Ten Commandments to Moses. Jews believe that this was the most important thing that has ever happened in the history of the world, because it was God explaining to people how he wanted them to live.

Before the festival begins, the synagogue is decorated with fruit and flowers. This is to remind people that, according to the **Torah,** Mount Sinai bloomed with flowers when God gave the Torah to Moses. It also symbolizes that the Shavuot is a harvest festival. At the synagogue service, there are readings from the holy books about how God gave the Ten Commandments to Moses. After the service, Jews celebrate with a meal at home. The meal includes two special loaves of **challah** bread with the pattern of a ladder baked into them. This is to remind people that Moses climbed the mountain to talk to God. Dairy foods are a traditional part of the Shavuot meal, too.

Purim

Purim is the story of King Ahasuerus—thought by some to have been Xerxes—and Queen Esther. They were king and queen of Persia—now modern Iran—in the fifth century B.C.E., when many Jews lived there. Ahasuerus had a chief minister named Haman, who insisted that everyone should bow to him. Jews considered bowing to be a sign of worship, and it was wrong to worship anyone except God. One day, a Jew did not bow as Haman walked past, so Haman became angry. He decided to get rid of all the Jews in Persia. He went to the king and told him that Jews were refusing to obey the laws of Persia. He persuaded the king to order that all Jews should be killed. Haman was superstitious. He decided to draw lots to find out what would be the best day for the killing. Purim is a word for "lots" and this gives the festival its name.

Queen Esther heard about Haman's plan. Although the king did not know it, she was a Jew. Queen Esther decided she must try to save her people. However, the king was all-powerful, and she was only supposed to see him when he sent for her. She invited Ahasuerus and Haman to a feast. This was a very brave thing to do. Esther was obviously very frightened, because before she asked to see the king she asked all Jews to **fast** and pray for three days and nights. During the feast, she told the king the real reason for what Haman was planning—that it was because the Jews would not bow to him. Ahasuerus was very angry, and he ordered that Haman should be killed instead. All the Jews were saved.

The day before Purim is a day of fasting for Jews, to remember that Esther asked the Jews to fast and pray before she spoke to Ahasuerus. Then there is a synagogue service in which the story is read. During the reading, children stomp their feet and whistle every time the name of Haman is mentioned. Sometimes they use special rattles called greggors. The idea is to make as much noise as possible to drown out Haman's name. Children often take part in plays telling the story, and there are costume parties and Queen Esther contests. Purim is also a time for giving to charity, and people give each other presents of food.

Giving to charity

Giving to people who are less fortunate is an important part of Judaism. Giving to others is an important part of the festival of Purim. However, Judaism teaches that giving charity should be done in a way that does not cause anyone embarrassment. At Purim, everyone, whether they are rich or poor, gives food to others. In this way, everyone can give and receive without feeling embarrassed. In Jewish teachings, there is a difference between giving money or gifts to other people and giving of your time. Judaism teaches that if you are giving money, it is better to give so that no one knows who has made the gift. Giving of your time and effort is very important in Jewish communities. Friends and neighbors generally help others if someone is ill, needs a babysitter, and so on.

Festivals—Hanukkah

Hanukkah is sometimes called the Festival of Lights. It falls in December, from Kislev 25th to Tebet 2nd, and lasts for eight days. At Hanukkah, Jews remember a story from their history.

The story of Hanukkah

The events that Jews remember at Hanukkah happened in Jerusalem almost 2,000 years ago. A cruel emperor named Antiochus was ruling the Jews' country. He refused to let the Jews worship God, and demanded that they worship him instead. The Jews knew that to worship this man would break the most important Jewish commandment, which says that Jews must not worship anyone or anything but God.

▲ *Even very young children can enjoy the festivities of Hanukkah.*

A group of Jews decided to fight against Antiochus. They formed a guerrilla army that fought in secret against the soldiers of Antiochus. They were led by a man named Judah Maccabee. Maccabee was his nickname. It is the **Hebrew** word for "hammer."

After three years of fighting, Judah and his friends captured Jerusalem. This meant they had gained control of the **Temple,** the most important building in the Jewish religion. Antiochus had wanted to make the Temple unfit for Jews to use for worship. He had ordered a statue to be set up there and said that Jews should make sacrifices to it. Those who refused were tortured or killed. This **idol**-worship made the Temple unclean. "Unclean" meant that it was far more than just dirty. It meant that the Jews could not use the Temple to worship God until it had been specially cleaned and made holy again.

When Judah was in control in Jerusalem, one of the first things he did was order the Temple to be made a fit place in which to worship God again. This was obviously a difficult job. The stories say the Temple had been abandoned and grass was growing through the floor.

When it was ready, the Temple lamp was lit. This was a special lamp that was supposed to burn all the time, but Antiochus had let it go out. Judah and his friends found that there was only enough oil for it to burn for one night. The oil was special and it would take eight days to get more. But when the soldiers returned after eight days with the new oil, the lamp was still lit. The people said that it was a miracle. They believed that God had made the lamp stay lit to show how pleased he was that he could be worshiped in the Temple again. Judah and the soldiers also realized that this miracle showed that their victories had been miracles, too. Their tiny army had conquered Antiochus and all his soldiers. They felt that they could only have achieved this with God's help.

▼ *Children play the dreidel game.*

Celebrating Hanukkah

In the celebrations for Hanukkah, Jews use a special candlestick called a **menorah.** It holds eight candles, plus another one called a shamash. The shamash is used to light all the others. On the first night of the festival, Jewish families say special prayers and light the first candle. On the second night, they light two candles, and so on. By the end of the festival all nine candles burn brightly to show that the Jews are remembering the miracle of how the oil lasted. The menorah often is placed in the window so that it can be seen clearly and gives light in the darkness. Although it is not one of the most important festivals, Hanukkah is a very happy time, especially for children. There are often parties, and people give each other presents. They eat special foods such as doughnuts and latkes—potato cakes—fried in oil.

The dreidel game

There is a traditional game that Jewish children play at Hanukkah. It is called the dreidel game. A dreidel is similar to a spinning top with four flat sides. On each side there is a Hebrew letter. They spell the first letters of the words that mean "a great miracle happened here." Outside Israel, the last word is "there" not "here." The letters are Nun (נ), Hey (ה), Gimmel (ג), and Shin (ש).

When the game starts, there is a "bank" of candies or counters in the middle. If the dreidel falls on Nun, you do nothing. If it falls on Hey, you take half the candy. If it falls on Gimmel, you take all of them. If it falls on Shin, you put candy back. Players add to the bank if it empties. The game ends when a player wins all of the candy.

Family Occasions—Childhood

Bris

When a Jewish boy is eight days old, he is **circumcised.** This procedure may be performed by a rabbi in a ceremony called a "Bris." Afterward, there is usually a party for the child's family and their friends.

Bar mitzvah

Bar mitzvah means "son of the commandments." On a **Sabbath** around his thirteenth birthday, a boy is called to the reading desk in the synagogue to recite the blessing on the **Torah** before it is read. Most read a part or even the whole of the sidra, the section of the Torah that is that day's reading. To read the **Hebrew** well enough to do this takes a lot of practice, especially when the boy is nervous at the idea of reading in front of a lot of people! In many **Orthodox** synagogues, the boy is also given his own **tefillin** for the first time, and so he must learn how to put them on before the service.

After the boy has finished his reading, his parents sometimes give a brief talk. In this they thank God that the boy has grown up and say that he is now counted as an adult. In some synagogues, the boy replies. Usually, the **rabbi** congratulates the boy and gives a little talk for his benefit.

After the service, there is usually a celebration meal for the boy's family and friends who have come to the synagogue to support him. He is given presents—often books that will help him to learn more about Judaism. A popular gift is a Jewish prayer book, called a **Siddur.** Once he has become bar mitzvah, a boy is counted as an adult in everything involving his religion. He can be counted as one of the **minyan,** the ten men who are necessary before a full synagogue service can be held. He also is expected to obey all of the Jewish laws.

▲ *A boy celebrates his bar mitzvah at the Western Wall.*

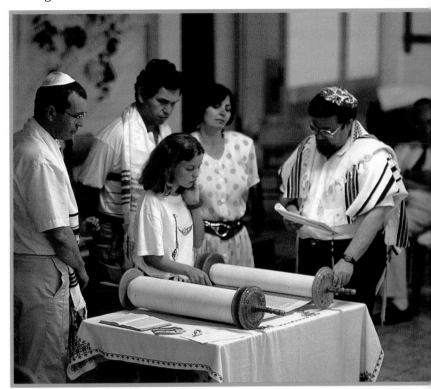

Bat mitzvah

Bat mitzvah means "daughter of the commandments." A girl becomes bat mitzvah automatically at the age of twelve. Traditionally, Jewish girls did not have a celebration to mark their bat mitzvah. Now, many Jews do have a celebration, but the form it takes can be very different in the different traditions. Orthodox synagogues that hold a service for girls hold it on a Sunday rather than on the Sabbath. Girls do not read from the Torah in an Orthodox synagogue.

In **Reform** and **Conservative** synagogues, there is no difference between the services held for boys and girls. There is usually a party for family and friends after the service.

Many synagogues hold **bat chayil** ceremonies for girls. This means "daughter of excellence." Sometimes the girls prepare for the ceremony by learning more about Judaism and perhaps doing a project on some aspect of Judaism that particularly interests them. In the ceremony, the girls read a passage in Hebrew and are welcomed by the congregation.

Jacob's view

Jacob, 13, lives in Melbourne, Australia.

My bar mitzvah was earlier this year. Of course, you know for years that when you turn thirteen you will become bar mitzvah, and I was looking forward to it. But when it came to the Sabbath after my birthday, when I had to do the reading, I was scared stiff! The **Temple** was nearly full, and when I walked up to the reading desk, I was really shaking. I was sure everyone could hear my heart beating. Then when I started reading, everything was OK. I'd practiced it a lot, and I knew everything really well, so I could just do it automatically. When I got to the end, I felt a bit flat. It was all over. Then we had the meal and I got some great presents. So by the end, I felt I'd had a really good day. Now I enjoy the feeling that I'm a full member of the congregation, and I can be one of the minyan. I don't find keeping all the Jewish laws that difficult at the moment. We've always kept them at home, and I go to a Jewish school so I'm surrounded by people who live in the same way. Things might be a bit more difficult when I leave home, but being Jewish is so important to me that I can't see me ever changing that much.

Family Occasions—Marriage and Death

As in other religions, many Jews believe that it is not really possible to share a life happily with someone who has not been brought up to follow the same faith and traditions. Therefore, many Jews would not consider marrying someone who is not Jewish. Others do not believe this is so important. In the last 50 years, increasing numbers of Jews have married "outside" Judaism.

▲ *A couple celebrate an outdoor wedding in Israel.*

The marriage service

Jewish marriages usually take place in the synagogue, although they can be held in other places. In Israel, they often are held outdoors. The ceremony is conducted by a **rabbi.** In **Orthodox** communities, the couple **fast** until after the wedding service. They pray and ask forgiveness for things that they have done wrong. This is so that they can start the new stage of their life with a "clean slate."

Wherever the wedding takes place, the couple stand underneath a **huppa.** This is a special canopy that may be beautifully decorated with flowers. It is a symbol of the home that the couple will share. The service begins when the rabbi repeats a blessing over a cup of wine. He or she then gives the cup to the bride and groom to drink. Then the **ketubah** is read. This is a marriage **covenant.** The bridegroom gives the bride a ring, which she wears on the first finger of her right hand. As he gives it to her he says, "With this ring you are sanctified to me according to the Law of Moses and Israel." The rabbi then thanks God for creating human beings and for bringing happiness to the couple. At the end of the service, the groom breaks a glass by stepping on it. It is wrapped in cloth to make sure that it does not do any damage. This is a very old custom and it has many meanings. It reminds the couple that there may be bad things as well as good things in life, and that they must face them together. It is also a reminder of the destruction of the **Temple.**

As soon as the wedding service has ended, the bride and groom go into a separate room. They spend a few minutes together and have something to eat if they have fasted before the service. Then they go back to the wedding guests for the rest of the celebration. In the past, and still in some traditional communities, the celebration lasted a week. The bride and groom were invited to different people's homes every night to be the guests at a special meal.

Divorce

Jews allow divorce, but they usually go to great efforts to save a marriage. Friends and relatives try to help the couple sort out their difficulties. If divorce cannot be avoided, a **get** must be issued. This is a certificate of divorce. It must be written on **parchment** by a trained scribe. It gives all the details of the couple and of where and when they divorced. This is the only way that a Jewish marriage can be ended. A civil divorce—one granted by a court of law—does not end a Jewish marriage, except in Israel, where the civil divorce is the Jewish divorce. Once the get has been issued, in Jewish law, either person is free to remarry.

Death

Jews believe that a funeral should take place soon after death, if possible within 24 hours. Funerals are very simple, as Jews believe that rich and poor should be treated alike. After all, death happens to everyone. Jews do not normally allow cremation, as they believe it destroys what God has made. The time of formal mourning is called Shiva and lasts for a week. During this time, the mourners do not leave home. Friends and members of the synagogue visit them three times every day to offer prayers and comfort them.

Jewish burial customs

Traditionally, the body of a Jewish person is prepared for burial by members of a *chevra kaddisha*. This is a "burial society" that is made up of volunteers. Men prepare male bodies and women prepare female bodies. Preparing someone's body for burial is counted as a great responsibility. It also is seen as being the greatest kindness possible, because the person can never repay it. A Jew's body must not be buried wearing makeup or fine clothes. The body is washed and wrapped in a plain linen **shroud.** Then it is placed in a plain wooden coffin. Rich and poor are treated in exactly the same way.

▶ *A Jewish cemetery on Mount Kidron overlooks Jerusalem.*

What It Means to Be a Jew

In the community

Many Jews choose to live in areas where there are other Jews. The rules about observing the **Sabbath** mean that strict **Orthodox** Jews need to live within a short walking distance of the synagogue. They need to attend Sabbath synagogue services, but they may not walk far, drive a car, or use public transportation on that day. Living in a community of Jews means that shops cater to Jewish customers. There are likely to be specialty food shops, and supermarkets are more likely to sell **kosher** food. Most important, it enables Jews to mix with other Jews, people who share their religious traditions and ideas. Community groups are more likely. For example, many Jews like their children to spend at least some of their time with other young Jews, and playgroups or youth clubs can be important meeting places.

At the synagogue

Orthodox Jewish men go to the synagogue as often as they can for the daily prayers. Attendance at Sabbath services and festivals is even more important. In addition to the formal services, Jewish men and women often attend the synagogue for classes that teach them more about the **Torah** and the Jewish way of life.

▲ *These Jews are meeting for study in a **rabbi's** home.*

In the home

For many Jews, life at home is a very important part of their faith. The customs that they follow may have been handed down for generations. Being careful with the preparation of food—which they believe has been given by God—is one way of serving him. This is how the rules about kosher food fit into the pattern of life—not as rules that are there for the sake of it, but as a way of living that serves God.

Eating food, too, is a reason for thanking God. Many Jews recite special blessings for particular foods. For example, before eating fruit, they say, "Blessed are you O Lord our God, King of the universe, who creates the fruit of the tree." For many Jews, blessing God in almost every situation in which they find themselves is so much a part of life that it is second nature.

▼ *Jews prepare food very carefully to make sure it is kosher.*

Keeping kosher

Kosher means "allowed." It is the way that Jews describe things that are fit and proper. Many Jews only eat kosher food. Anything that is not kosher is **treif,** which means "forbidden." All plants are kosher, provided they do not have pests or "creepy-crawlies" on or in them. Not all animals and birds are kosher. Animals with a cloven hoof that chew the cud—such as cows and sheep—are kosher. Scavenger animals such as crabs are strictly forbidden. Some birds are allowed. Jews today eat chicken, turkey, and duck. Fish are permitted if they have fins and scales.

To be kosher, an animal has to be killed by having its throat cut with a razor-sharp knife, so that it does not feel pain. The Torah forbids causing any animal to suffer. Meat also must be soaked in salt so that all the blood is removed before it is cooked. Meat and dairy products are not eaten together. So, for example, Jews do not put butter on a meat sandwich or serve a pudding or custard after a meal that included meat. Jews have observed these rules for thousands of years. For Jews, careful preparation of food and thanking God for it by following the rules they believe he gave are important parts of their daily religion.

Map

The globe on the right shows the location of the map below.

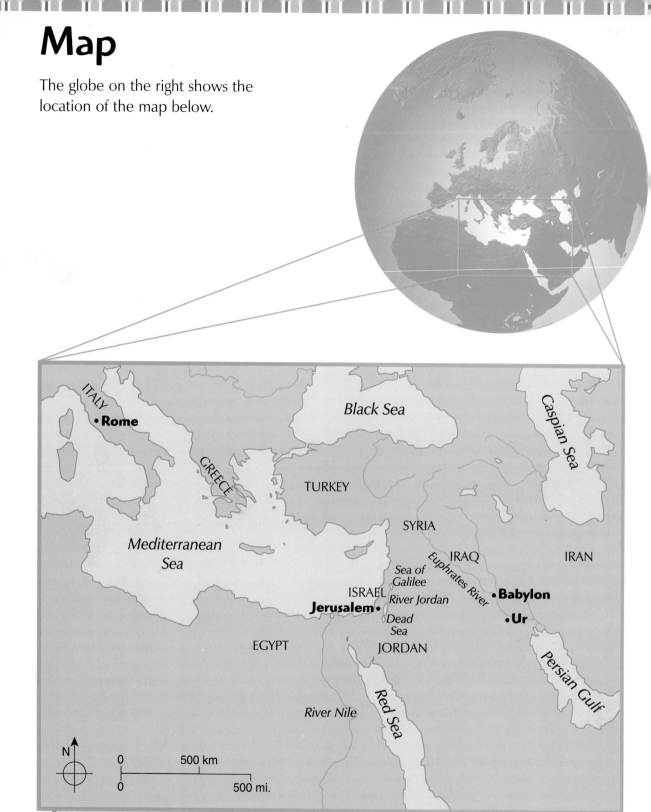

Place names

Some places on this map or mentioned in the book have different names today:

Assyria—ancient kingdom ca.1400–600 B.C.E. centered around Northern Iraq and Southeast Turkey

Babylon—ruins are 56 miles (90 km) south of Baghdad, Iraq

Babylonia—ancient region based around southern Iraq ca.1850 B.C.E.–540 C.E.

Palestine, Canaan—Israel

Persia—Iran

Ur—Tall-al-Maqayar, Iraq

Timeline

Major events in world history

Major events in Jewish history

Glossary

Adonai	"Lord"—Jewish name for God
adultery	sexual relations outside of marriage
ark	special cupboard in the synagogue where scrolls are kept
Bar mitzvah	"son of the commandments"—ceremony for Jewish boys
Bat chayil	"daughter of excellence"—ceremony for Jewish girls
Bat mitzvah	"daughter of the commandments"—ceremony for Jewish girls
bet din	Jewish court
cantor	person who sings parts of the service in the synagogue
challah	bread specially baked for the Sabbath and holidays
circumcised	to have the foreskin removed from the penis
concentration camp	one of several guarded prison camp where Nazis held and killed millions of members of minority groups during World War II
Conservative	branch of Judaism that accepts the challenge of changes to Jewish life
convert	to become a member of a religion in which you were not raised
Covenant	solemn agreement;agreement between God and the Jews
covet	to be jealous of what someone else owns
Day of Atonement	day on which Jews ask forgiveness for their sins
Deuteronomy	fifth book of the Torah, which includes the teaching Moses gave to the Israelites; also part of the Christian Bible
Diaspora	name given to the spread of Jews around the world
eternal	lasting forever
Exodus	second book of the Torah, which includes the escape from Egypt and the time in the desert; also the name for the time when the Jews escaped from Egypt
fast	to go without food and drink for religious reasons
Genesis	first book of the Torah, which tells of the creation of the world and early Jewish history
get	certificate of Jewish divorce
Hasidic	group of Orthodox Jews who follow strict Jewish laws about marriage, food, dress, and religious life
Havdalah	ceremony and prayers that end the Sabbath
Hebrew	traditional Jewish language
Holocaust	persecution and killing of Jews during World War II
huppa	canopy under which Jewish weddings take place
idols	something someone worships instead of God, such as a statue or even a possession
Israelites	early name for the Jews
Judges	early leaders of the Jews; also a chapter of the Christian Bible
ketubah	marriage document
Ketuvim	"holy writings"—third section of the Jewish holy books
kosher	"fit"—food that Jews may eat
Leviticus	third book of the Torah, which tells about Temple worship and festival observance; also part of the Christian Bible
lulav	collection of palm, willow, and myrtle branches plus a citrus fruit used at Sukkot to remind Jews to worship God with their entire bodies
mantle	decorative covering for scrolls

matzoh	unleavened bread
menorah	eight-branched candlestick, similar to the lamp that burned in the Temple
Messiah	"promised one" whom Jews believe will come to establish God's kingdom
mezuzah	pronounced meh-ZOO-zah; tiny scroll for placing on a doorpost
minyan	group of ten Jews, necessary for a full synagogue service
Mishnah	collection of the teachings of rabbis about the Torah
mitzvot	commandments—rules that Jews should follow
Nazis	members of the National Socialist Party, in power in Germany during the 1930s and 1940s
ner tamid	everlasting light—a lamp in the synagogue
Nevi'im	the Books of the Prophets—second section of the Jewish holy books
Numbers	fourth book of the Torah, which tells of counting the Israelites and some Jewish history
Orthodox	branch of Judaism whose members strictly follow the Torah
parchment	material made of animal skin on which the Torah is written
Pesah	pronounced pay-soch; another name for Passover
Pharaoh	ancient Egyptian king
pilgrimage	journey for religious reasons
prophets	messengers from God
Psalms	poems that are part of the Jewish holy books and Christian Bible
rabbi	Jewish teacher and leader
Reform	branch of Judaism begun in Germany in the eighteenth century
Sabbath	Saturday; Jewish day of rest and worship
Seder	"order"—the Passover meal
Sefer Torah	Torah scroll
shofar	ram's horn used in Jewish worship on Rosh Ha-shannah and Yom Kippur
shul	common name for synagogue
shroud	large piece of cloth used to wrap a dead body
Siddur	Jewish prayer book
Sukkah	more than one are called sukkot; a hut or tent used during the festival of Sukkot
Tabernacles	Jewish festival of tents, also known as Sukkot
tallit gadol	prayer shawl used for worship
tallit katan	fringed garment worn under ordinary clothes
Talmud	collection of Jewish law and teachings
tefillah	more than one are called tefillin; leather boxes worn by Orthodox Jewish men on their arms and foreheads
Temple	most important place of Jewish worship, destroyed by the Romans in 70 C.E.; also name used by Reform Jews in the U.S. for synagogue
Tenakh	name for the complete Jewish holy books
Torah	Books of Teaching—first section of the Jewish holy books
treif	pronounced tray-eff; food that is forbidden, or not kosher
yad	Hebrew word for "hand"; the pointer used when reading a Torah scroll
yarmulka	pronounced yahr-mull-keh; skullcap worn by many Jewish men and some women

More Books to Read

David, Jo. *The Book of the Jewish Life*. New York: U.A.H.C. Press, 1997.

Diner, Hasia. *Jews in America*. New York: Oxford University Press, 1998.

Wood, Angela. *Jewish Festivals*. Chicago: Heinemann Library, 1997.

Index